The Minimum Wage: No Way to Help the Poor

DEEPAK LAL

James S. Coleman Professor of International Development Studies
University of California at Los Angeles

THE INSTITUTE OF ECONOMIC AFFAIRS
1995

First published in January 1995

by

THE INSTITUTE OF ECONOMIC AFFAIRS
2 Lord North Street, Westminster, London SW1P 3LB

© Institute of Economic Affairs 1995

Occasional Paper 95

ISSN 0073-909X

ISBN 0-255 36344-3

Cover design by David Lucas

Printed in Great Britain by
GORON PRO-PRINT CO LTD, LANCING, WEST SUSSEX
Set in Plantin 11 on 13 point

Contents

Foreword

MANY COUNTRIES SET MINIMUM WAGES, despite the common claim by economists that such devices are ineffective means of relieving poverty – indeed, that they hurt those they are intended to help by increasing unemployment among the young and the unskilled. Recently, however, signs of a split in the economics profession on this issue have appeared: the case for a minimum wage has been revived both in the United States and Europe.

In *Occasional Paper* No.95, Professor Deepak Lal of the University of California at Los Angeles reviews these 'revisionist' studies, placing them in the context both of the relevant theory and of empirical work.

Professor Lal's starting point is George Stigler's seminal paper in 1946 which argued that, given the adverse effects on employment of a minimum wage, a better way of helping the poor is to subsidise their incomes directly. Subsequent empirical research has, in Lal's view, produced a 'virtual professional consensus that a minimum wage is a poor anti-poverty device'. He shows also that studies of both developed and developing countries demonstrate that setting or increasing minimum wages increases unemployment.

New arguments for a minimum wage are, however, based on efficiency rather than poverty-relief grounds. The case is that in a labour market where an employer has monopsony power – of which one example is the 'company town' – wages will be set below the competitive level. If they are raised to that level by a minimum wage, both employment and efficiency can evidently be increased.

As Professor Lal observes, whether or not one takes these arguments seriously depends on whether or not it can be shown that monopsony in labour markets (hitherto generally regarded by economists as a 'theoretical *curiosum*') is in practice widespread. But he can find no such evidence in the new studies.

The one new idea which Professor Lal finds is that of 'dynamic monopsony' which does not rely on the existence of 'company towns'. It is based on the assumption that, even in labour markets where there are many small employers, there is a monopsonistic element because workers have imperfect information about job opportunities. It is claimed that, in such circumstances, imposition of a minimum wage would increase efficiency.

Lal questions the 'monopsony' label for such circumstances and argues that the authors are undertaking an exercise in 'Nirvana economics': implicitly they are comparing an apparently 'imperfect' labour market with the perfectly competitive ideal. As he points out, it is most unlikely that in real labour markets, wages will be equated with the marginal product of labour. Employers and employees adapt to uncertainty in various ways which make divergences inevitable: their existence 'does not provide a case for the distortion introduced by a minimum wage'.

In real-world labour markets, Lal argues, there would be numerous side-effects of a minimum wage. In particular, he instances the impact on human capital formation: because a minimum wage tends to reduce the dispersion of wages, it will reduce the incentive to acquire skills. Thus support for a minimum wage is 'at odds with [the] desire to promote skill accumulation by unskilled workers – particularly the young and females'.

Professor Lal concludes his devastating critique of 'revisionist' minimum wage ideas by pointing out that even if the labour market were 'riddled with monopsony, the requisite information that the technocrats would require to correct it is unavailable...there is no obvious technocratic solution which would be better than that discovered by the market'. So the minimum wage should be regarded as 'an inefficient, well-intentioned but inexpert interference with the mechanisms of supply and demand'.

The Institute publishes this *Occasional Paper* as an important contribution to the revived debate about minimum wages. The views expressed are, of course, those of the author, not of the Institute (which has no corporate view), its Trustees, Directors or Advisers.

January 1995   COLIN ROBINSON
Editorial Director, Institute of Economic Affairs;
Professor of Economics, University of Surrey

Acknowledgements

This paper was written whilst I was a Fellow of the International Centre for Economic Research in Turin. Comments by two anonymous referees on the draft are gratefully acknowledged.

January 1995   D.L.

The Author

DEEPAK LAL is James S. Coleman Professor of International Development Studies, University of California at Los Angeles, and Professor Emeritus of Political Economy, University College, London. Born in 1940, and educated at the Doon School, Dehra Dun, St Stephen's College, Delhi, and Jesus College, Oxford, he has been a member of the Indian Foreign Service (1963-66), Lecturer, Jesus College, Oxford, and Christ Church, Oxford (1966-68), Research Fellow, Nuffield College, Oxford (1968-70), Lecturer and Reader in Political Economy, University College, London (1970-84), and Professor of Political Economy, University of London (1984-93). He was a full-time consultant to the Indian Planning Commission during 1973-74, a visiting fellow at the Australian National University, 1978, and has served as a consultant to the ILO, UNCTAD, OECD, UNIDO, the World Bank, and the ministries of planning in South Korea and Sri Lanka. During 1983-84 he was an Economic Adviser to the World Bank, and then Research Administrator (1984-87), on leave from University College, London.

Professor Lal is the author of numerous articles and books on economic development and public policy including: *Unemployment and Wage Inflation in Industrial Economies* (1977); *Men or Machines* (1978); *Prices for Planning* (1980); (with P. Collier) *Labour and Poverty in Kenya* (1986); *The Hindu Equilibrium* (2 vols., 1988, 1989); and he has edited (with M. Wolf) *Stagflation, Savings and the State – Perspectives on the Global Economy* (1986). Two collections of his essays have recently been published: *The Repressed Economy* (1993) and *Against Dirigisme* (1994). The IEA has published his *The Poverty of 'Development Economics'* (Hobart Paperback No.16, 1983), and his Wincott Memorial Lecture, *The Limits of International Co-operation* (IEA Occasional Paper No.83, 1990).

The Minimum Wage: No Way to Help the Poor

DEEPAK LAL

1. Introduction

LIKE A BAD PENNY, every so often, controversy about the minimum wage returns despite the considerable body of agreement amongst economists – until recently – that as Samuelson's famous textbook put it:

> '[A]s Adam Smith well knew when he protested against the devices of the mercantilist advisers to the earlier kings, most economic systems are plagued by inefficiencies stemming from well-intentioned inexpert interferences with the mechanisms of supply and demand. A few such interferences [are]: 1. Minimum wage rates. These often hurt those they are designed to help. What good does it do unskilled black youths to know that an employer must pay him $4·00 per hour if that fact is what keeps them from getting jobs.'[1]

Samuelson then goes on to list rent and price ceilings and usury laws as other examples of these 'inexpert interferences' in the working of the price mechanism. But now the minimum wage is back on the agenda in Britain (as part of the Labour Party's economic programme) and other European countries and the United States.

Its proponents will be heartened by some recent studies which seek to overturn the existing consensus amongst economists that the minimum wage is not an efficient instrument to deal with the problem it seeks to solve. This problem, as traditionally viewed by its advocates, is poverty: their idea is to alter the distribution of income at the lower end of the spectrum in the hope that poverty will be alleviated.

---

[1] P.A. Samuelson, *Economics*, 11th edition, New York: McGraw Hill, 1980, p.369.

But with the shock administered to egalitarians by the collapse of 'really existing socialism', as well as the diminishing appeal of their ethic to Western electorates, some economists have come to base the case for their favourite 'social' programmes on grounds of economic efficiency rather than as traditionally on those of equity.[2] And so it is with the minimum wage. It is now being claimed that a minimum wage can improve the efficiency of a market economy!

This paper first briefly reviews the traditional case for the minimum wage as an instrument of poverty alleviation (Section 2), before examining the theoretical and empirical arguments behind the efficiency case (Section 3). A final section provides some general conclusions.

Single National Minimum or Industry-Based Minima

At the outset it is useful to note that minimum wages can either take the form of a single national minimum or be set differentially for different groups in different industries. In the USA the 1938 Fair Labor Standards Act established a single national minimum wage. In France too the SMIC (*'salaire minimum interprofessionnel de croissance'*), established in 1950, provides a single national minimum.

By contrast, in the UK there has been a multiplicity of legal minimum wages. They were first instituted by the Trade Boards Act of 1909 in four industries which were purported to have 'sweated labour'. These boards were transformed into wages councils after the Second World War. Until 1986 these wages councils set a number of minimum hourly wages for different types of workers within their industries. Following the Wages Act of 1986 they were allowed to set only a single basic minimum wage for the

---

2 Thus see for instance the case made for the welfare state by N. Barr, 'Economic Theory and the Welfare State: A Survey and Interpretation', *Journal of Economic Literature*, Vol.XXX, No.2, June 1992, pp.741-803. For counter-arguments why this case is an example of what Harold Demsetz ('Information and Efficiency: Another Viewpoint', *Journal of Law and Economics*, Vol.12, No.1, 1969) has termed 'nirvana economics' see D. Lal, 'The Role of the Public and Private Sectors in Health Financing', UCLA Dept. of Economics Working Paper No.717, July 1994.

workers in their jurisdiction and workers under 21 were removed from that jurisdiction. All wages councils, except in agriculture, have now been abolished.

Moreover, as Kaufman noted:

'[A]lthough those industries covered by the wages councils are typically among the lowest paying industries in the country, it is not true that most low-paid workers are covered. The *Royal Commission on the Distribution of Income and Wealth* defined a low-paid male (female) as someone whose earnings place him (her) in the lowest decile of all male (female) workers. It is estimated that only 11 per cent of all full-time low-paid males and 19·2 per cent of all full-time low-paid females were employed in industries covered by wages councils in the mid-1970s. Furthermore, only 18 per cent of the manual men covered by wages councils were low paid compared with 87 per cent of the women.'[3]

Not surprisingly, the current controversy, in the USA and in Britain, is about the desirability of a *single* national minimum wage. The British Labour Party, for example, proposes to introduce a *national* minimum wage to cover all low-paid workers.

2. Poverty Alleviation

IT HAS SEEMED intuitively plausible to many politicians and the untutored that low pay as determined by the market is a cause of poverty, and hence the 'cure' – that is, raise their wages to a 'living wage' – has had continuing resonance. [4] The *locus classicus* of the economist's retort is Stigler's 1946 article. [5] He pointed out:

---

[3] R.T. Kaufman, 'The Effects of Statutory Minimum Rates of Pay on Employment in Great Britain', *The Economic Journal*, Vol.99, No.398, December 1989, p.1,042

[4] See D.O. Parson, 'Minimum Wages', in *The New Palgrave: A Dictionary of Economics*, Vol.3, London: Macmillan, 1987, pp.476-78.

[5] G.J. Stigler, 'The Economics of Minimum Wage Legislation', *American Economic Review*, Vol.36, June 1946, pp.358-65.

- *First*, that a minimum wage would reduce employment in the sectors of the economy that were covered (unless the particular labour market was monopsonistic – on which more below, p.18), and that this fall in employment could outweigh the rise in wages, leading to lower earnings for the 'poor'.

- *Second*, unless the low paid were also the poor, or the fewer jobs at a 'living wage' were rationed to poor families, there was no guarantee that they would not in practice merely benefit the low-wage members of wealthier households, such as teenagers.

- *Third*, as the sectors uncovered by the minimum wage would have to absorb those unable to find jobs in the covered sectors, their wages could fall, offsetting any poverty alleviation gains in the covered sectors. If the whole economy is covered, of course, this 'excess' labour created by the minimum wage would be unemployed, or would have to leave the labour force.

Stigler's 'Second-Best' Solution

Hence Stigler advocated what has come to be accepted as the central principle of 'second-best' welfare economics, *viz*. if there is a 'distortion' in the working of the market mechanism – in this case a divergence of the incomes the 'low paid' receive compared to what the community thinks they ought to receive – it is best to go to the heart of the matter, which in this case would be to subsidise their incomes directly. Creating another 'distortion' in the working of the labour market through a minimum wage would be 'second best', and only relevant if the direct remedy were infeasible. [6] As most Western economies run

---

[6] For a brief outline and application of this type of 'second-best' welfare economics in a variety of contexts see D. Lal, *The Poverty of 'Development Economics'*, Hobart Paperback No.16, London: Institute of Economic Affairs, 1983.

elaborate welfare states, clearly this last condition is not met, and hence the minimum wage *is* an inefficient way to deal with the problem of 'low-wage' poverty.

Subsequent empirical research, done largely for the United States, has confirmed the validity of Stigler's views. Thus a recent study by Burkhauser and Finnegan which examined, from 1939 to 1987, the relationship between poverty and the hourly wage of workers earning less than the median wage found that

> 'save for unrelated individuals, the link between how much a worker earns per hour and the economic well being of his or her household is now almost completely lost – and along with it the target efficiency of minimum wage legislation'. [7]

Another study by Lineman concluded that

> 'the burden of the minimum wage falls most severely on females. This effect on adult females is surprisingly neutral with respect to race. The greatest beneficiaries of the minimum wage among the adult population are union members. Once again, this effect is relatively neutral with respect to race'. [8]

Thus it would be fair to say there is a virtual professional consensus that a minimum wage is a poor anti-poverty

---

[7] R.V. Burkhauser and T.A. Finnegan, 'The Economics of Minimum Wage Legislation Revisited', *Cato Journal*, Vol.13, No.1, Spring 1993, p.127. An earlier study by Gramlich also concluded that the correlation between wages and family income was a loose one, so that 'minimum wages will never have strong redistributive effects. For every billion dollars that a boost in the minimum brings to low-wage workers, $0·3 billion goes to teenagers, who either do not benefit at all or who are so spread out along the distribution as to prevent effective income redistribution. Of the $0·7 billion received by adults, 25 per cent goes to families with incomes above the median, requiring 25 per cent to families with incomes below the median just to cancel the distributional impact of this leakage, and leaving only half as a net absolute gain to the latter group. Hence this net gain from the minimum wage boost is only $350 million. When it is recalled that the 25 per cent increase in the minimum wage in 1974 added only 0·4 per cent to the aggregate wage bill, its redistributive impact of 0·14 per cent of the wage bill (0·4x0·35=0·14) easily gets lost in the shuffle.' (E.M. Gramlich, 'Impact of Minimum Wages on Other Wages, Employment and Family Incomes', *Brookings Papers on Economic Activity*, No.2, 1976, pp.445-49.)

[8] P. Lineman, 'The Economic Impacts of Minimum Wage Laws: A New Look at an Old Question', *Journal of Political Economy*, Vol.90, No.3, June 1982, p.443.

device. As Milton Friedman has put it in his characteristic way:

> 'Many well-meaning people favour legal minimum-wage rates in the mistaken belief that they help the poor. These people confuse wage *rates* with wage *income*...Moreover, many workers in low-wage brackets are supplementary earners – that is, youngsters who are just getting started or elderly folk who are adding to the main source of family income. I favour governmental measures that are designed to set a floor under *family income*. Legal minimum wages only make this task more difficult.'[9]

3. Efficiency

THE DIRIGISTES HAVE, however, opened a different front. As Stigler had noted that, if (in an otherwise perfectly competitive economy) the labour market was not competitive and employers had some monopsony power, such that they could pay workers less than the value of their marginal product, then a minimum wage set at the competitive level would increase employment, and thence the efficiency of the economy (by equating the wage with the value marginal product of labour in the monopsonistic industry – see Figure 1 below).

But monopsony in the labour market has always been considered to be, by and large, a theoretical *curiosum*. Thus the last general survey of the literature on the minimum wage noted – and then only in a footnote – that

> 'the textbook exception of the monopsonist whose employment rises in response to a skilfully set minimum wage has little impact on the minimum wage literature outside textbooks, in large part because the company town is not (if it ever was) the context of most minimum wage employment'.[10]

---

[9] M. Friedman, 'Minimum Wage-Rates', Reading No.51 in P. Samuelson, J.R. Coleman and F. Skidmore (eds.), *Readings in Economics*, New York: McGraw Hill, 1967, p.259.

[10] C. Brown, 'Minimum Wage Laws: Are they overrated?', *Journal of Economic Perspectives*, Vol.2, No.3, September 1988, p.134, n.1. An earlier survey by C. Brown, C. Gilroy and A. Cohen, 'The Effect of the Minimum Wage on Employment and Unemployment', *Journal of Economic Literature*, Vol.XX,

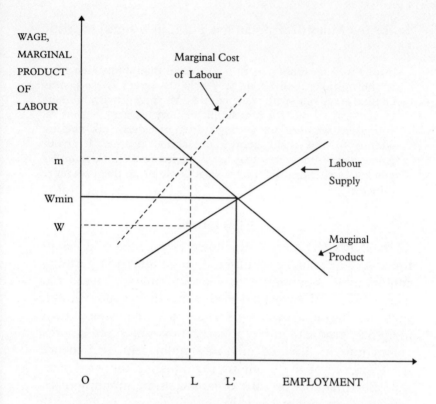

FIGURE 1: Employment Effects of a Minimum Wage

Note: In a competitive labour market, the market wage would be Wmin and employment OL'. Under monopsony the employer equates the marginal cost of hiring labour with its marginal product (m), employing OL workers at the wage rate W, which is less than the marginal product. A minimum wage set at the wage rate Wmin, increases employment by LL', and also equates the wage with the marginal product of labour. If the minimum wage is set higher than Wmin, then employment starts contracting from the competitive level.

But the monopsony case is now being revived! [11]

No.2, June 1982, provided a more detailed analysis of the monopsony case (see p.489).

[11] That monopsony may exist in some labour markets is well known. Thus in their textbook, R.B. McKenzie and G. Tullock (*Modern Political Economy*, New York: McGraw Hill, 1978) discuss monopsony in relation to the employer cartel in professional football in the USA, and the employment rules governing faculty in

Theorists also noted that when complications were introduced into the model, then even without monopsony, the effects of minimum wages were in principle ambiguous. Thus Harry Johnson[12] showed that it was even possible that workers in the sector uncovered by the minimum wage could be better off, contrary to Stigler's argument. This could happen if the sector covered by the minimum wage was more capital-intensive than the uncovered sector. With the minimum wage, if the demand for the capital-intensive covered sector's output was fairly elastic, its employment and output would tend to fall. This would release not only labour but also capital for use in the labour-intensive industry but, *ex hypothesi*, in proportions which would increase the overall capital intensity and hence wages in the uncovered sector (as it would be receiving more capital relative to labour from the declining covered industry).

Unemployment Effects of Minimum Wages

Similar theoretical ambiguities attend analyses of the unemployment effects of minimum wages.[13] The simplest case is one commonly found in many developing countries. There, minimum wages are usually applicable (and if universal are only enforceable) in the so-called 'formal' or modern sector of the economy. This artificial raising of wages in the 'formal' sector causes a rise in unemployment as workers in the 'informal' sector search for these newly desirable high-paid jobs. But the actual method of search will determine the extent of unemployment that will result.[14]

---

the 16-campus University of North Carolina system (see their Ch.15). But as we shall see below, such employer cartels are more difficult to set up in precisely those industries where it is now claimed there is evidence of dynamic monopsony.

[12] H.G. Johnson, 'Minimum Wage Laws : A General Equilibrium Analysis', *The Canadian Journal of Economics*, Vol.II, No.4, November 1969.

[13] See J. Mincer, 'Unemployment Effects of Minimum Wages', *Journal of Political Economy*, Vol.84, No.4, Pt.2, August 1976.

[14] J.R. Harris and M.P. Todaro, 'Migration, Unemployment and Development: A two-sector analysis', *American Economic Review*, Vol.60, No.1, March 1970;

Given these theoretical ambiguities, it is not surprising that empirical evidence is needed on the employment effects of minimum wage laws. In the early 1980s, a Democratic-controlled US Congress issued a report on the minimum wage, as did the American Enterprise Institute.[15] Eccles and Freeman provide a useful summary table comparing the findings of the two studies (reproduced in the Appendix, below, pp.32-38).[16] As they note, there seemed surprising agreement in the two studies on the impact of the minimum wage on, for instance, the distribution of income, employment, unemployment, and non-wage effects on job-training.

Most of these effects have been estimated by econometric methods. On the employment effects, a small negative impact of the minimum wage on youth employment is found. Summarising this evidence, Brown *et al.* conclude that 'a 10 per cent increase in the minimum wage reduces teenage employment by one to 3 per cent'.[17] For the UK, Kaufman estimated '-0·06 as the approximate total employment elasticity'[18] for the statutory minimum wages of the wage councils. For France, Bazen and Martin's best estimate of the effects of the SMIC on youth employment is an employment elasticity in the range 'from -0·1 to -0·2 which spans the consensus values found in the American and British literature'.[19]

G.S. Fields, 'Rural-Urban Migration, Urban Unemployment and Underemployment, and Job-Search Activity in LDCs', *Journal of Development Economics*, Vol.2, No.1, 1975, reprinted in D. Lal, *Development Economics*, Vol.1, Aldershot: Edward Elgar, 1992.

[15] US Congress, *Report of the Minimum Wage Study Commission*, 7 vols., Washington DC, July 1981; S. Rottenberg (ed.), *The Economics of Legal Minimum Wages*, Washington DC: American Enterprise Institute, 1981.

[16] M. Eccles and R.B. Freeman, 'What! Another Minimum Wage Study?', *American Economic Review*, Vol.72, No.2, May 1982, pp.226-32.

[17] Brown *et al.* (1982), *op. cit.*, p.524.

[18] Kaufman, *op. cit.*, p.1,052.

[19] S. Bazen and J.P. Martin, 'The Impact of the Minimum Wage on Earnings and Employment in France', *OECD Economic Studies*, No.16, Spring 1991, p.215.

One reason why the employment effects of the minimum wage seem so small in these econometric studies is the limited effectiveness of the relevant minimum wages. Thus in the USA, despite periodic hikes in the minimum wage, in 1988 its value relative to average earnings was 0·36 compared to 0·56 in 1968. Trying to estimate the very marginal effects of very marginal changes in this 'distortion' is not likely to provide persuasive evidence of the impact of an effective minimum wage on employment. Better examples are provided by studying a number of developing countries which have used minimum wage laws to subserve various objectives.

Dramatic Effect of Minimum Wages: Puerto Rico and Singapore

The most dramatic example of a reduction in employment caused by the enforcement of minimum wage laws was the extension of the US Fair Labor Standards Act to Puerto Rico (a low-wage area) soon after the Second World War. Reynolds and Gregory estimated that employment forgone was about 8,000 workers between 1949 and 1954 when employment in manufacturing was 58,000 in 1950, and 29,000 workers in the 1954-58 period when manufacturing employment was 66,000 in 1955.[20] Similarly, there was a large contraction in employment in Florida when the law was applied during the same period.[21]

An equally impressive contraction in output and employment occurred when Lew Kuan Yew, from motives very different from the usual poverty-alleviating ones, raised wages in Singapore in 1979, by nearly 20 per cent a year for three years.[22] He wanted Singapore to move rapidly

---

[20] L.G. Reynolds and P. Gregory, *Wages, Productivity and Industrialization in Puerto Rico*, New Haven, Con.: Yale University Press, 1965, p.304 and Table 1-5.

[21] See M.R. Colberg, 'Minimum Wage Effects on Florida's Economic Development', *Journal of Law and Economics*, Vol.3, October 1960.

[22] In 1972 the Singapore government had set up a tripartite National Wages Council to formulate annual wage guidelines. 'These guidelines are not mandatory, but they are fully implemented in public firms and strongly

towards high-tech industries, and sought to 'persuade' producers to do so, by artificially raising the price of their labour. The result was

'a substantial increase in unit labour costs, which reduced Singapore's international competitiveness in relation to that of other Asian NIE's and contributed to the 1985 recession and to the accompanying decline in manufactured exports and employment'.[23]

In many other developing countries the minimum wage has been close to the lowest market-determined wage (for example, in many Latin American countries),[24] or else it has not been enforced. In such cases it has, in effect, been redundant. Even in the United States, as noted above, the legal wage minimum has been fairly low; not surprisingly, economy-wide studies have found the employment effects to be negative, but small.

New Empirical Studies Based on Monopsony Model

Some recent empirical studies have sought to overturn this conventional wisdom. Two are noteworthy: one for the USA by Card and Krueger and the other for the UK by Machin and Manning.[25] Both base themselves on a monopsonistic model of the labour market – the theoretical *curiosum* identified by Stigler.

Unlike the company town, where the only employer can plausibly be expected to exercise some monopsonistic power over his workers, we are now told that the fast food labour market (from the evidence cited) is monopsonistic in

---

influence wage settlements in private enterprises.' (R. Findlay and S. Wellisz (eds.), *The Political Economy of Poverty, Equity and Growth: Five Small Economies*, New York: Oxford University Press, 1993, p.115.)

[23] *Ibid.*, p.116.

[24] See P. Gregory, *The Myth of Market Failure: Employment and the Labour Market in Mexico*, New York: Oxford University Press, 1986.

[25] D. Card and A.B. Krueger, 'Minimum Wages and Employment: A Case Study of the Fast-Food Industry in New Jersey and Pennsylvania', *American Economic Review*, Vol.84, No.4, September 1994; and S. Machin and A. Manning, 'The Effects of Minimum Wages on Wage Dispersion and Employment: Evidence from the UK Wage Councils', *Industrial and Labour Relations Review*, Vol.47, No.2, January 1994.

the USA, as are those for catering, retailing and clothing in the UK – and which were covered by the 26 Wages Councils which after 1986 set a single basic minimum wage for their workers. Brown *et al.* note:

> 'One "test" of the monopsony model is to determine whether it is common for a small number of employers to employ a majority of the workers in a labour market. Robert Bunting's 1962 study of 1,774 labour markets (most "labour markets" being counties) found that the four largest employers employed at least half of the semi- and unskilled workers in less than 3·7 per cent of the labour markets.'[26]

No such 'test' is provided to judge the plausibility of the assumption of monopsony in the labour markets cited in the new revisionist literature.[27] Nor, even within the confines of their limited objective of demonstrating that (as in the case of monopsony) a rise in the minimum wage causes an increase in employment in the covered sectors, are the results robust.

Thus, consider Card and Krueger's study of fast-food restaurants in New Jersey and eastern Pennsylvania, before and after the rise in New Jersey's minimum wage in April 1992 from $4·25 to $5·05. They find that, compared with restaurants in eastern Pennsylvania where the minimum wage remained unchanged, and with those in New Jersey which were already paying over the new minimum wage, the restaurants affected by the rise in the minimum wage in New Jersey *increased* their employment – at a time when the economy was in a recession. This would be in consonance with the monopsony model.

But whereas that model would predict that the affected restaurants would also reduce their product prices, Card and Krueger found instead that prices of fast-food meals increased in New Jersey relative to Pennsylvania (which

---

[26] Brown *et al.*, *op. cit.*, p.489, n.2. The reference to Bunting is to R.L. Bunting, *Employer Concentration in Local Labour Markets*, Chapel Hill, N.C.: University of N. Carolina Press, 1962. It studies the United States.

[27] But see below (p.21) for the justification provided by one of these studies for the applicability of this type of model.

would conform to the competitive view of the labour market). However, 'within New Jersey, [they find] *no* evidence that prices increased more in stores that were most affected by the minimum wage rise', because they conjecture fast-food stores in New Jersey 'compete in the same product market', and so the restaurants affected by the minimum wage cannot increase their prices faster than their competitors. They conclude:

> 'Taken as a whole, these findings are difficult to explain with the standard competitive model or with models in which employers face supply constraints (e.g. monopsony or equilibrium search models).'[28]

This hardly provides any robust justification for the monopsony viewpoint in favour of the minimum wage.[29]

'Dynamic Monopsony'

The second study by Machin and Manning is of the UK wages councils. They argue that the modern theory of

---

[28] Card and Krueger, *op. cit.*, p.792

[29] In a forthcoming book (Card and Krueger, *Myth and Measurement - The New Economics of the Minimum Wage*, Princeton, New Jersey: Princeton University Press, 1995), Card and Krueger also look at the past studies (including the Reynolds-Gregory study of Puerto Rico noted above, p.17) of the employment effects of minimum wages. They conclude that 'Our reading of the evidence from Puerto Rico is that it is remarkably *indecisive* on the question of whether higher minimum wages have a large negative effect on employment' (p.264). Their conclusion on past US studies of the minimum wage is that 'under close scrutiny, the bulk of the empirical evidence on the employment effects of the minimum wage is shown to be consistent with our findings...which suggest that increases in the minimum wage have had, if anything, a small, positive effect on employment, rather than an adverse effect' (p.236). They also include six other new studies including cross-section studies covering the 50 US states of the 1990 and 1991 increases in the minimum wage. Their conclusion from all this is that: 'The absence of negative employment effects in all the studies...provides reasonably strong evidence against the prediction that a rise in the minimum wage leads to a fall in employment. Although *most of the estimated employment effects are insignificantly different from zero*, the results are uniformly positive, and relatively precisely estimated' (p.389, emphasis added). On the poverty alleviating effects of the minimum wage they conclude that: 'On balance, our conclusions echo those of Gramlich' (p.308) which we noted above (p.12), show the effects to be minimal. Finally, in their search for an explanation of their findings they seem to side with the dynamic monopsonists (see their Ch.11).

'dynamic monopsony' does not need to rely on the example of company towns for its relevance.

> 'The basic idea of dynamic monopsony is that employers who pay higher wages face lower quit rates...and find it easier to recruit new workers. Hence there will be a positive relationship between the wage offered and the labour supply to the employer: this is of course the key distinguishing feature of the monopsony approach. The implicit assumption underlying this approach is that workers have imperfect information about the job opportunities offered by different employers. ... In contrast to traditional monopsony, modern monopsony is likely to be relevant in labour markets where there are many small employers since information about job opportunities is likely to be less easy to find out than in a labour market dominated by a few large employers.'[30]

By emotively labelling the complex market solutions to the ubiquitousness of risks associated with both labour supply and demand – which are due to imperfect information on both sides of the market – as 'dynamic monopsony', they are implicitly comparing it with the perfectly competitive ideal, and the associated notion of 'market failure'. This is, of course, an exercise in Nirvana economics[31] – as we shall see. Their empirical evidence in favour of the claim that 'modern monopsony suggests that a minimum wage policy may raise employment' consists of statistical regressions of changes in full-time employment of adults (that is, excluding youths and part-timers) in the

---

[30] Machin and Manning, *op. cit.*, p.320.

[31] Demsetz, *op. cit.*, defines 'nirvana economics' as follows: 'The view that now pervades much public policy economics implicitly presents the relevant choice as between an ideal norm and an existing "imperfect" institutional arrangement. This *nirvana* approach differs considerably from a *comparative institution* approach in which the relevant choice is between real institutional arrangements. In practice, those who adopt the nirvana viewpoint seek to discover discrepancies between the ideal and the real and, if discrepancies are found, they deduce that the real is inefficient. Users of the comparative institution approach attempt to assess which alternative real institutional arrangements seem best able to cope with the economic problem.' (H. Demsetz, *Efficiency, Competition and Policy*, Oxford: Blackwells, 1989, p.3.) Nirvana is of course the Hindu ideal of salvation!

industries covered by the Wages Councils during the 1980s, and changes in a measure of the 'toughness' of the minimum wage in the industry (given by the relevant minimum wage as a proportion of average earnings). If the competitive model holds, the relationship should be negative; in the case of monopsony, it should be positive. Dividing their wage councils into four broad groups – retail, clothing, catering and hairdressing – they find:

> 'for catering toughness has a significant positive association with employment. For retail and clothing the estimated effect is positive but insignificant while for hairdressing it is negative but insignificant.'[32]

Such results are hardly a resounding confirmation of their preferred 'dynamic monopsony' argument for minimum wages!

It should also be noted that, even on their own evidence, different minimum wages would be required for different industries to deal with their differing degrees of monopsony. A *single* national minimum wage could still affect some industries adversely, if this mimimum was above their competitive wage.

No Direct Evidence of Monopsony

Furthermore, no direct evidence relating to the structure of these industries is provided to demonstrate that they are monopsonistic. In fact, these industries are the very ones where, whatever the initial degree of monopsonistic power,[33] it is likely to be eroded over time. As McKenzie and Tullock argue:

> 'If a large number of employers each hires only a very small fraction of the total labour force, collusion is particularly

---

[32] Machin and Manning, *op. cit.*, p.327.

[33] Machin, Manning and Woodland ('Are workers paid their marginal product? Evidence from a low wage labour market', Centre for Economic Performance, London School of Economics, Discussion Paper No.158, July 1993) found that the 'rate of exploitation' in a sample of residential homes in England's 'sunshine coast', was 15 per cent - that is, their wages were 15 per cent less than their marginal product!

difficult. For instance, it is very difficult for owners of hot-dog and hamburger stands in large metropolitan areas to effectively collude on their individual demands for the types of workers they hire. If all employers manage to collude and decide collectively to reduce their demand for labour, the wage can fall. However, once the wage has fallen, there is an incentive for each firm to take advantage of the lower wage by expanding the number of workers employed. If the individual firm is small, an increase in employment will not alone materially affect the market wage rate. Furthermore, in a free market, new firms will enter the labour market to take advantage of the artificially low wage. In other words, each employer (each owner of hamburger stands) has an incentive to chisel on any collusive agreement in the labour market. If many employers chisel, competition will return, leading to increases in the market wage rate. Given the incentive to chisel, the cost of forming a workable cartel can be so great that no one will attempt to form one. This is typical of most labour markets; it is certainly characteristic of employers of workers for hamburger stands.'[34]

Finally, as Alan Walters has noted:

'In all the wages councils I investigated in 1981-84, the large employers were all enthusiastic supporters of the wages councils. If the monopsony explanation were true, then by supporting high and effective minimum wages, they would be reducing – indeed, in principle eliminating – their profits. The explanation lay in the fact that the large employers – often partly or wholly unionised – had conceded wages which exceeded those of their smaller competitors, mainly, one suspects, immigrant family-owned shops often staffed with family labour. These small competitors were adamantly opposed to minimum wage rules which may have bankrupted them and reduced employment and at least inhibited their (albeit mostly modest) expansion plans.'[35]

More seriously, the so-called dynamic monopsony argument ultimately boils down to an inferred divergence between the market wage and the marginal product of

---

[34] R.B. McKenzie and G. Tullock, *op. cit.*, pp.271-72.

[35] A. Walters, 'Unemployment: Subsidies and Minimum Wages', *Economic Affairs*, Vol.15, No.1, Winter 1994, p.50.

labour at a point in time.[36] It is well known that, except for casual labour markets characterised by spot contracting, such an equality is unlikely to exist in most other labour markets.[37] Because of uncertainty due to imperfect information – on both sides of the labour market – a variety of labour market contracts will exist to cope with these risks, and it is unlikely that they will conform to the perfectly competitive norm.

But, given that the associated uncertainty is irreducible – so that it cannot be reduced to the actuarial risk on which the technocrat's so-called Arrow-Debreu paradigm[38] is based – the implication is that these contracts arising from the discovery process of the market are likely to be 'constrained Pareto efficient'. Thus the divergence between market wages and value marginal products – on which the dynamic monopsony argument is based – does not provide a case for the distortion introduced by a minimum wage. The market outcomes we observe occur from various adaptations that participants make to deal with 'imperfections' in imperfectly competitive markets.

---

[36] This is clear from the formal model one set of revisionists present in R. Dickens, S. Machin, A. Manning, 'The Effect of Minimum Wages on Employment: Theory and Evidence from Britain', Centre for Economic Performance, London School of Economics, Discussion Paper No.183, January 1994. See in particular their equation 3.

[37] See, for instance, P. Collier and D. Lal, *Labour and Poverty in Kenya: 1900-1980*, Oxford: Clarendon Press, 1986, Ch.4.

[38] The Arrow-Debreu paradigm refers to the basic theorems of welfare economics, rigorously derived by Professors Arrow and Debreu. These show that, in a perfectly competitive economy with universal markets for all commodities distinguishable not only by their spatial and temporal characteristics but also by the various conceivable 'states of nature' under which they could be traded - that is, there is a complete set of futures markets for so-called 'contingent' commodities - a *laissez-faire* equilibrium will be Pareto-efficient in the sense that, with given resources and available technology, no individual can be made better off without someone else being made worse off. A 'contingent' commodity, for instance, would be 'labour' for delivery on 9 January 2000, where the future price is conditional on whether or not the demand for hamburgers is 20 per cent above average that month! The irrelevance of this paradigm for public policy is argued in Lal, 'Markets, Mandarins and Mathematicians', *Cato Journal*, Vol. 7, No.1, 1987, reprinted in Lal, *Against Dirigisme*, San Francisco: ICS Press, 1994.

Given the heterogeneity in the abilities and aptitudes of the labour force and the unavoidable risks associated with both labour supply and demand, one finds a multiplicity of labour market contracts developing in any real-world labour market, for seemingly similar types of labour.[39] These labour market contracts also have to take account of the differing costs and benefits associated with the general and firm-specific skills imparted by on-the-job training by firms. To judge these real world adaptations to the ubiquitous problems of imperfect information and irreducible uncertainty by the perfectly competitive norm is a case of 'nirvana economics'. So what would we expect to be the effects of a minimum wage in this more realistic world?

Since Machin and Manning, in the passage cited above (p.18), claim that it is the relationship between wage rates and quit rates which is the essence of 'dynamic monopsony', let us examine the question further for a very simple case where human capital formation in the form of on-the-job training is of importance. As is well known, the skills imparted by such training can be distinguished as 'general' and hence marketable outside the firm, and 'firm-specific' where their value lies only within the firm.[40]

On-The-Job Training

First, consider the case of on-the-job training which provides *firm-specific* skills.[41] In this case, the investment in skill acquisition has to be shared between the worker and the firm. The employer has an incentive to reduce the quit rate of workers who have acquired firm-specific skills (exactly as in the 'dynamic monopsonists' claim). Various

---

[39] See O.E. Williamson, *Markets and Hierarchies*, Glencoe, Ill.: Free Press, 1975.

[40] See G. Becker, *Human Capital*, 2nd edn., New York: Columbia University Press, 1975.

[41] A fuller and more rigorous discussion of what follows is to be found in Ch.4 and Ch.6.III of P. Collier and D. Lal, *op. cit.*

wage structures (normally incorporating some form of seniority scale), with a divergence between the wage and the marginal product of the worker, will be observed. They will be 'second-best' optimal, given that the employer cannot tie down a worker to whom he has imparted firm-specific skills (in the absence of indenture) without compelling him – through the structure of wages offered – to make an implicit investment in the firm which is later repaid.[42] So for a period the wage could be lower than the worker's marginal product, to be offset by a wage which is higher or equal to the marginal product in other periods.

Depending upon the particular but differing circumstances of the relevant industries, we would expect a multiplicity of such contracts in which the perfectly competitive labour market condition that wages are always equal to the marginal product of labour would not be met. Instead, there would usually be a divergence between wages and marginal products, as in 'dynamic monopsony'. But this 'distortion' in no way implies any dynamic inefficiency, given that firm-specific skills have economic value, and that without such contracts they would not be imparted.

Perhaps in such a labour market there could be a rise in the employment of workers whose wages are below their marginal product (as depicted by the monopsony case in Figure 1 – above, p.14), with the introduction of a minimum wage. But what might be the cost in terms of skill-acquisition, and thence the dynamic efficiency of the economy? One effect of the minimum wage will be to reduce seniority premiums, that is, to flatten the wage structure (or reduce wage dispersion).[43] This can be shown

---

[42] See, for instance, J. Stiglitz, 'Alternative Theories of Wage Determination: The Labour 'Turnover Model', *Quarterly Journal of Economics,* Vol.LXXXVIII, May 1974, reprinted in D. Lal, *Development Economics*, Vol.1 (of 4), Aldershot: Edward Elgar, 1992.

[43] This truncation of the wage structure is a common effect of the introduction of a minimum wage. See, for example, C.F. Thies, 'The First Minimum Wage Laws', *The Cato Journal*, Vol.10, No.3, Winter 1991. For the UK, Machin and Manning, *op. cit.*, bemoan the fact that as a result of the declining 'toughness' of

to lead to a rise in the cost of firm-specific training for the firm, and hence to lower skill acquisition.

The compression of wages induced by the minimum wage will also reduce the worker's incentives to incur the investment he requires for acquiring *general* skills. As these skills are marketable in other employment, the employer will not share in the costs of their acquisition. But the employer will have to raise the wage in line with the acquisition of skills or risk losing the worker to a competitor. For these reasons there will be a close relationship (equality in the case of perfect competition) between the wage and the marginal product of the worker.

Equally important, the accumulation of these general skills will be a positive function of skill-specific wage differentials. If with the compression of the wage structure – with the introduction of a minimum wage – these skill-specific wage differentials decline, there will be lower accumulation also of these general skills. So, irrespective of what happens to employment, these effects of the minimum wage on human capital accumulation from on-the-job training could seriously damage the dynamic efficiency of the economy.[44] Thus support for the minimum wage is at odds with another valid desire to promote skill accumulation by unskilled workers – particularly the young and females. Both the studies (by Hashimoto and Leighton and Mincer) summarised in the Appendix (below, p.38), which examine the effects on job-training of the minimum wage in the USA, found a negative effect (see also the Box on p.28).

---

the Wages Councils' minimum wages, there has been an increase in the dispersion of wages in the covered industries. Card and Kreuger (in *Myth and Measurement, op. cit.*) also find for the USA that 'the 1990 and 1991 increases in the minimum wage led to a significant compression of wages in the lower tail of the overall wage distribution - effectively rolling back as much as 30 per cent of the increased wage inequality that developed during the 1980s' (p.308).

[44] It should be noted that in his authoritative study Mincer found that the on-the-job training component of the investment in human capital in the United States was a third or more of the total, the rest being accounted for by formal education. (J. Mincer, *Schooling, Experience and Earnings*, New York: Columbia University Press, 1974.)

Measures for an Employment Policy Package

Two other measures which have been advocated as part of an 'employment policy' package are the regulation of non-wage conditions of employment and the introduction of wage subsidies, particularly for the unskilled and the long-term unemployed.

On the former, current legislative initiatives in the EU to limit freedom of contracts (e.g. maximum hours worked) can be even more deleterious than minimum wages.[1] For the USA, J. Gruber[2] found that the costs of mandated maternity benefits were entirely shifted to the 'beneficiaries' so that the pay of the affected group (married women of child-bearing age) fell. If minimum wages had prevented this adjustment in pay, presumably more of the group would have been unemployed.

With the public-policy-induced rise in unemployment in many OECD countries arising from such well-meaning labour market interventions, many are now arguing for *wage subsidies* to offset the effects of these labour market distortions – particularly for the unskilled and the long-term unemployed.[3] This resurrects an argument familiar to students of developing countries. In fact, I spent part of my misguided youth in estimating such 'shadow wages' for many developing countries,[4] where because of trade union pressure an effective minimum industrial wage had limited the amount of industrial employment of unskilled labour, whose true social cost – the 'shadow wage'– it was argued was lower than the market wage industrial employers had to pay. The difference between the market and 'shadow' wage was the required wage subsidy.

No developing country I advised, followed this advice – in part because of administrative feasibility, and more importantly because of the realistic fear that the political process which had led to the 'distortion' in the first place, would merely lead to the shifting of the subsidy to existing industrial labourers, with no net effect on the employment of the 'outsiders'. With the general move from the plan to the market in many developing countries, they have instead as part of their liberalisation packages sought to do, what developed countries should emulate, namely, to remove the policy-induced distortion! But as Alan Walters notes,[5] there was some justification for introducing the 'Young Workers Scheme' before the Thatcher trade union reforms were in place as a temporary expedient to deal with the existing 'policy-induced' distortion in the working of the youth labour market.

---

[1] See J.Addison and S. Siebert, *Social Engineering in the European Community: The Social Charter, Maastricht and Beyond*, IEA Current Controversies, No. 6, London: Institute of Economic Affairs, July 1993.

[2] 'The Incidence of Mandated Maternity Benefits', *American Economic Review*, June 1994.

[3] See, for example, E.S. Phelps, 'Low wage employment subsidies versus the welfare state', *American Economic Review*, May 1994.

[4] See, for instance, D. Lal, *Prices for Planning*, London: Heinemann Educational Books, 1981.

[5] 'Unemployment: Subsidies and Minimum Wages', *Economic Affairs*, Vol 15, No. 1, Winter 1994.

Stronger evidence is found in a case that Paul Collier and I studied in detail, that of Kenya.[45] It is of relevance because the bulk of the labour market of a developing country is in many ways similar to the much smaller (relative to the size of the economy) unskilled or low-skilled markets in developed countries. We can therefore observe the effects of minimum wages on the wages structure and thence on skill acquisition more starkly in these developing countries than in the more marginal unskilled labour markets of developed countries.

Between the mid-1950s and late-1960s the urban minimum wage was raised very sharply in Kenya, more than doubling in real terms between 1954 and 1962, largely on the humanitarian grounds of providing African urban workers with a 'living wage'. In our detailed study of Kenyan labour markets, where we took account of the imperfections emphasised by the 'dynamic monopsony' school, we attempted to see what the effects were. The employment effects were swamped by a general boom in African employment following Independence. But we found that

> 'the increase in the minimum wage had a powerful effect upon the wage structure, reducing the pace of skill accumulation, especially among manual workers. ... Second, to the extent that the minimum wage increase did succeed in raising the wage level it induced an increase in urban job-search unemployment. The extension in 1967 of the minimum wage to all those aged eighteen and over exacerbated youth unemployment in particular'.[46]

Thus we concluded that

> 'the distorting effect [of the minimum wage] on labour allocation might have been primarily upon a reduction in the

---

[45] See P. Collier and D. Lal, *Labour and Poverty in Kenya: 1900-1980*, Oxford: Clarendon Press, 1986.

[46] *Ibid.*, p.167.

net accumulation of human capital rather than upon the level of employment, or more particularly, upon the level of unemployment'.[47]

4. Conclusions

A DESIRE TO INTERFERE in the working of the labour market has always been the Achilles' Heel of socialism. It reflects atavistic attitudes that wages should be regulated by 'justice' rather than by supply and demand. At one time the Roman Catholic Church seemed to share the same view.[48]

But this is a very slippery slope. As Phelps Brown argues, such views lead naturally to the Webbs' recommendation that under socialism:

'the "present competitive determination of wages" would be superseded "by their assessment by public authority on the basis of the Standard of Life necessary for full efficiency". The structure of pay would be made up of a national minimum and, mounted on that, a differential for each occupation, assessed according to its particular requirements'.[49]

Given the evident failure of the latter part of the schema in 'really existing socialism', socialists have reluctantly abandoned the detailed planning of wages advocated by the Webbs, but still cling to its base – the national minimum. It is like the Cheshire Cat – with now nothing left but the grin. But will the full cat return?

Such impulses have been buttressed by technocratic notions based on the 'nirvana' approach to public policy. They are not new. The famous debate in the 1930s about the feasibility of central planning was, after all, sparked off by Oscar Lange and Abba Lerner's assertion that a planned economy could simulate a perfectly competitive economy and hence achieve the most efficient and distributionally

---

[47] *Ibid.*, p.171.

[48] As set out in the encyclicals *Rerum Novarum* (1891), *Quadragesimo Anno* (1931) and *Mater et Magistra* (1961).

[49] E.H. Phelps Brown, *The Economics of Labour*, New Haven, Con.: Yale University Press, 1962, pp.197-98.

just outcomes, which were inconceivable in any actual market economy riddled with various forms of 'market failure'. The stance of our younger Lange-Lerners, who seek to introduce minimum wages to redress the inefficiencies of the 'dynamic monopsony' they see all around them in the labour market, is of a similar ilk.

But the antidote provided by Hayek in the earlier debate is as relevant in this current controversy.[50] Even if we accept that the labour market is riddled with monopsony, the requisite information that the technocrats would require to correct it is unavailable. What is more, when account is taken of the other indirect purposes served by so-called 'dynamic monopsony', for instance in on-the-job-training and in dealing with the myriad other irreducible uncertainties on both sides of the labour market, there is no obvious technocratic solution which would be better than that discovered by the market.

The revived controversy over the minimum wage thus reflects the continuing hold of certain atavistic impulses combined with a continuing lack of understanding amongst technocrats of the workings of an actual as compared with an idealised market economy. Despite the passions aroused, the textbook conclusion with which we began – that the minimum wage is an inefficient, well-intentioned but 'inexpert interference' with the mechanisms of supply and demand – still stands.

---

[50] See Lal, *The Poverty of 'Development Economics'*, *op. cit.*, for a brief outline of this debate.

APPENDIX

TABLE 1 - COMPARISON OF MINIMUM WAGE STUDIES: MINIMUM WAGE
STUDY COMMISSION vs. AMERICAN ENTERPRISE INSTITUTE

1. Demographic Profiles and
   Compliance

A. MWSC

Gilroy

48% of all minimum wage workers are 16-24 years old. 37% are women 25 years and over, relatively large proportions of minimum wage workers in groups of: teenagers 16-17 (62%), 18-19 (33%), workers over 65 (39%), women (18%), blacks (18%), students (56%), part-time workers (36%), and poverty families (43%); only 9% of adults 20-64.

Institute for Social Research

1980 survey of low-wage establishments finds almost half of near-minimum wage workers under 20, the majority white, though a higher proportion of non-white workers in low-wage work than overall, higher proportion in the South.

Sellekaerts & Welch

In 1973-80, found non-compliance consistently higher in low-wage sectors, and in the South, among females, non-whites and teenagers than in complementary groups. In 1979 violation survey non-South's rate exceeds South's: overtime violations most prevalent. In 1978 *CPS* sample, overtime provisions violated at least in part 73% of the time.

Ehrenberg & Schumann

Considerable non-compliance with overtime pay provisions: overtime pay yields greater benefits to middle and upper-income families than to lower-income families; increases in overtime differential will create modest number of jobs.

B. AEI

Knesser

Using *CPS,* finds over 60% of all low-wage workers are female; under 40% are teenagers, 30% are in families below the poverty level, tendency to live in the South of Great Plains regions.

Bell

30% of low-wage workers are not household heads; concentration in families above the poverty level.

[32]

Fleisher

D.O.L retail trade surveys in 1962, 1965-66 shows over 90% compliance for U.S., lower rates in South, from 71% in 1962 to 87% in 1966 (in eligible workers covered).

Ehrenberg & Schumann

Same basic conclusions as in Ehrenberg and Schumann above.

2. Employment Effects - In
   General

A. MWSC

Abowd & Killingsworth

Under an *ad hoc* model a 2% increase leads to a 0·2 to 2·4% drop in teenage employment, a 0·2% rise to a 0·8% drop for adults. Under a structural model, a 2% increase leads to a 0·5% to 1% drop for teenagers, a negligible drop for adults.

Madden & Cooper

No statistically significant results as to interstate distribution of sales or employment in wholesale and retail trade.

Brown, Gilroy, Kohen

Survey of low-wage sector effects finds little conclusive evidence of adverse employment effects.

Heckman & Sedlockek

Using South Carolina worker data, a 20% minimum wage increase makes over 80% of S.C. workers worse off, either through disemployment or lower wages.

B. AEI

Wessels

Minimum wage significantly increases labour force participation of young adult females and males over 65, significantly decreases labour participation for young males, all with relatively small elasticities.

Trapani & Moroney

For seasonal cotton farm workers in late 1960s, 63% of large drops in employment attributed to extended minimum wage coverage.

[33]

Krumm

Significant disemployment effects in all localities on lowest-skill workers as they are replaced by medium-skilled, new labour market entrants.

Gardner

For farm workers, a rise of 5% in mean hourly wage leads to a minimum 5% reduction in employment.

Fleisher

In retail trade in the 1960s, given a labour cost rise of 5%, labour demand dropped 5%; expansion of employment in department stores relative to rest of retail trade.

Gordon

No significant effects on private household worker employment.

3. <u>Employment Effects for Youths and Youth Subminimum</u>

A. MWSC

Meyer & Wise

Without minimum wage, employment of non-student young men would be up 6% at least, average youth wage lower with the minimum.

Brown

Size of effects of youth differential on teenage and especially adult employment uncertain; problems with restricted differential.

Brown, Gilroy, Kohen

Survey of youth employment studies shows reasonably consistent time-series results that 10% minimum wage increase causes a 1 to 3% reduction in employment for 16-19 year olds, less consistency for 20-24 year olds and subgroups: their runs show a 0·5 to 1·5% drop.

Pettengill

Eliminating minimum for youths would increase employment among youth, indeterminate impact on non-youth low-wage workers.

Hamermesh

In private non-farm sector, a 10% minimum wage increase leads to a 1·2% drop overall: higher in manufacturing, lower in services and retail trade. Estimates that a 25% youth differential would increase employment by about 3%.

Freeman, Gray, Ichniowski

Student subminimum has led to an increase in student person hours worked by perhaps 17% at a cost of perhaps 1% of employment of full-time non-student worker hours.

B. AEI

Cunningham

For whites, employment is reduced, part-time work discouraged, and school attendance reduced, non-robust results for blacks.

Ragan

Legal minimum raises wages in youth-intensive sectors; some evidence that manpower programs have raised employment, that minimum reduces employment for some teenage groups.

Al-Salam, Quester & Welch

Expansion of coverage of minimum wages has reduced proportion employed by 0·4 and created a gap between black and white teenagers of roughly 0·04 as well; cohort size is important determinant of proportion employed.

Fleisher

In retail trade, significant negative impact on employment for young males, inconclusive results for females.

Mattila

For 14-19 year olds, significant results on increase in school enrollments, roughly equal to magnitude of decrease in non-student labour force.

Cotterill

Review suggests significant problems of exclusion of other low age groups by differential to youth, especially in retail and service areas.

Cotterman

Study of 18-19 year old males gives insignificant results for disemployment, except for significant in retail trade ($.25 increase leads to 25% drop in black employment, 16% in white); inter-industry shifts occur, with high-skilled teens; employment chances improved.

4. Income Distribution
A. MWSC

Behrman, Taubman & Sickles

In checking proportions falling below the poverty line, inconclusive results by race; females appear to do slightly better than males; varied results for other age-sex schooling groups.

Johnson & Browning

Through simulations, found even distribution of benefits over all income levels and disemployment effects lowering the benefits, generally small distributional effects, within income classes inequity increases (80% of low-income households lose because of higher prices, 10% of high-income households gain income).

Kohen & Gilroy

Found no strong correlation between individual earnings and family income, and therefore only small 'positive' effects on income distribution. Even distribution across income levels of minimum wage workers.

Datcher & Loury

Using *CPS* data, 20% increase in minimum wage causes white family earnings to rise over 1%, black earnings 0·2%; higher-income families gain absolutely none.

B. AEI
Parsons

Using *NLS*, found small wage gains for low-wage adult females, offset by employment reductions; amount to less than $150 per year.

McCulloch

Using Gini index, net negative effect on equality.

5. Macroeconomic Aspects

A. MWSC

Pettengill
1% minimum wage increase leads to a 0·3 to 1·3% of workforce forced out of labour market; average wage rise of 1 to 2%.

Farber
10% change in minimum leads to less than 0·5% change in union wage.

Boschen & Grossman
Increases in minimum wage depress current employment in some industries, no effect on aggregate employment or average wage rate; effect of indexation uncertain.

Cox & Oaxaca
10% rise leads to a 0·1% rise in aggregate real wage bill; an increase in high-wage employment, decrease in low-wage and overall.

Sellekaerts
10% minimum wage increase causes a rise of 0·05% in unemployment rate and 0·76% rise in average wages; initial impact of indexation uncertain: later effect beneficial (e.g. increased efficiency).

Wolff & Nadiri
Raising minimum wage has positive effect on output due to income distribution, negative on employment, and raises prices more rapidly as minimum rises.

B. AEI

McCulloch
Direct effect on inflation negligible, even if minimum wage is indexed.

6. Non-wage Job Effects
   (On-the-Job Training, etc.)

A. MWSC

Lazear & Miller
Using *NLS*, no obvious retardation effects of the minimum wage on wage growth.

B. AEI

Fleisher

Using *NLS*, while wage rates are higher in covered than non-covered sectors, adding the wage advantage of working to reported wages causes wages in uncovered sector to exceed those in covered sector for students and non-students.

Hashimoto

Using *NLS*, some reduction in On-the-Job Training (OJT) (2·5%) found for young white males; inconclusive results for blacks.

Wessels

Minimum wages have slight negative or neutral effects on labour participation, slight effects on priors, and a positive or neutral effect on quit rates.

Leighton & Mincer

Minimum wages discourage OJT especially at lower education levels; mixed results on job turnover.

Sources: Papers reviewed are contained either in Volumes II-VII of *The Report of the Minimum Wage Study Commission* (MWSC), published in July 1981; in the American Enterprise Institute's (AEI) conference volume, *The Economics of Legal Minimum Wages*, Simon Rottenberg (ed.), published 1981; Donald Parsons, *Poverty and the Minimum Wage*; Belton Fleisher, *Minimum Wage Regulation in Retail Trades*; Masanori Hashimoto, *Minimum Wages and On-the-Job Training*; Walter Wessels, *Minimum Wages, Fringe Benefits and Working Conditions*; or Ronald Krumm, *The Impact of the Minimum Wage on Regional Labor Markets*. In the Appendix, studies are referred to by author. *NLS* refers to the National Longitudinal Survey ('Parnes Survey') funded by the Department of Labor.

This Appendix was first published as Table 1 in M. Eccles and R.B. Freeman, 'Government Economic Policy Assessment: The Labor Market. What! Another Minimum Wage Study?', AEA Papers and Proceedings, in *American Economic Review*, Vol. 72, No.2, May 1982.

ECONOMIC AFFAIRS

The journal of the IEA

Spring 1995

Financial Regulation issue

(edited by Professor Harold Rose)

Main Articles

Individual issue £2.50

Annual subscriptions:

UK & Europe: £15.00 (Institution); £10.00 (Individual);
Rest of the World: £20.00/$35.00 (Surface); £30.00/$50.00 (Air)

Please apply to:

The Institute of Economic Affairs
2 Lord North Street, Westminster
London SW1P 3LB
Telephone: 071-799 3745: Fax: 071-799 2137

The End of Macro-Economics?
DAVID SIMPSON

1. The distinguishing feature of developed market economies is incessant qualitative change. New consumer and capital goods, and new methods of production and distribution are continuously being created and old ones destroyed.

2. Macro-economics looks at economic activity in terms of aggregates and averages. It obscures rather than assists an understanding of the essential features of economic activity in a market economy.

3. Macro-economics makes unwarranted assertions about the stability of empirical relationships between aggregates, assumes their unchanging composition, abstracts from essential elements of economic acitivity, and uses concepts out of context.

4. It is impossible to predict to what extent an increase in aggregate demand will be reflected in price rises and to what extent in output increases. In order to know what significance to attach to a numerical value for any aggregate, one has to disaggregate.

5. Aggregate concepts such as the NAIRU, the quantity of money, the output gap and competitiveness are all misleading, and have contributed to the implementation of unsuccessful and sometimes harmful policies.

6. Almost 20 years since it was publicly acknowledged that a government could not spend its way out of a recession, it has been discovered that the fine-tuning of bank lending does not work either. In the UK the operation of monetary policy has been uncoupled from macro-economic theory.

7. The cycle is an intrinsic part of the deregulated developed market economy and one cannot have the benefits of growth without it.

8. Repeated surveys have shown the complete failure of all attempts at short-term forecasting using macro-economic models. Only pattern predictions are possible.

9. Macro-economic theory is a dead-end in the history of economic thought. The way forward is to return to the classical tradition which emphasises the importance of uncertainty, innovation, entrepreneurship and institutional evolution, and has quite different policy implications.

10. Policies to approach full employment must facilitate the adaptation of workers from old jobs to new jobs. Taxes should be shifted from employment to consumption and subsidies should shift from unemployment to the search for, and acceptance of, new employment.

ISBN 0-255 36338-9

Hobart Paper 126

The Institute of Economic Affairs
2 Lord North Street, Westminster
London SW1P 3LB
Telephone: 071-799 3745

£8.00 inc. p.+p.